12163

P9-CDF-298

'Tis the Season

A CLASSIC ILLUSTRATED
CHRISTMAS TREASURY

Compiled by Cooper Edens

chronicle books · san francisco

We are on our way to the Realm of Sharing and Mystery.
My friends, enjoy! Friends! Enjoy!
—C. E.

Compilation © 2003 by Starsnap Studio.
All rights reserved.

The excerpt from *A Child's Christmas in Wales* by Dylan Thomas © 1954 by
New Directions Publishing Corp. is reprinted by permission of New Directions
Publishing Corp. World and English rights held by David Higham.

Book design by Donna Linden.
Typeset in Adobe Jenson and Mona Lisa.
Manufactured in Hong Kong.

Library of Congress Cataloging-in-Publication Data
'Tis the season : a classic illustrated Christmas treasury / compiled by Cooper Edens.
p. cm.
ISBN 0-8118-3768-8
1. Christmas-Literary collections. I. Edens, Cooper.
PN6071.C6 T57 2003
808.8'0334—dc21
2002014627

Distributed in Canada by Raincoast Books
9050 Shaughnessy Street, Vancouver, British Columbia V6P 6E5

10 9 8 7 6 5 4 3 2 1

Chronicle Books LLC
85 Second Street, San Francisco, California 94105

www.chroniclekids.com

I heard the bells on Christmas Day
Their old familiar carols play,
And wild and sweet
The words repeat
Of peace on earth, good-will to men!
—Henry Wadsworth Longfellow

Contents

Deck the Hall

· traditional welsh carol ·

Deck the hall with boughs of holly,
'Tis the season to be jolly,
Don we now our gay apparel,
Troll the ancient yuletide carol.

See the blazing yule before us
Strike the harp and join the chorus,
Follow me in merry measure,
While I tell of yuletide treasure.

Fast away the old year passes,
Hail the new, ye lads and lasses,
Sing we joyous, all together,
Heedless of the wind and weather.

O Come, All Ye Faithful

· john francis wade and frederic oakeley ·

O come, all ye faithful,
Joyful and triumphant,
O come ye, O come ye, to Bethlehem.
Come and behold Him, born the King of angels.
O come, let us adore Him,
O come, let us adore Him,
O come, let us adore Him,
Christ, the Lord.

Sing, choirs of angels,
Sing in exultation;
Sing all ye citizens of heav'n above:
Glory to God in the highest.
O come, let us adore Him,
O come, let us adore Him,
O come, let us adore Him,
Christ, the Lord.

Yea, Lord, we greet Thee,
Born this happy morning;
Jesus, to Thee be glory giv'n;
Word of the Father, now in flesh appearing.
O come, let us adore Him,
O come, let us adore Him,
O come, let us adore Him,
Christ, the Lord.

A Visit from St. Nicholas

• clement c. moore •

'Twas the night before Christmas, when all through the house
Not a creature was stirring, not even a mouse;
The stockings were hung by the chimney with care,
In hopes that St. Nicholas soon would be there.

The children were nestled all snug in their beds,
While visions of sugar-plums danced in their heads;
And mamma in her 'kerchief, and I in my cap,
Had just settled our brains for a long winter's nap,

When out on the lawn there arose such a clatter,
I sprang from the bed to see what was the matter.
Away to the window I flew like a flash,
Tore open the shutters and threw up the sash.

The moon on the breast of the new-fallen snow
Gave the lustre of mid-day to objects below;
When, what to my wondering eyes should appear,
But a miniature sleigh and eight tiny reindeer,

With a little old driver, so lively and quick,
I knew in a moment it must be St. Nick.
More rapid than eagles his coursers they came,
And he whistled, and shouted, and called them by name:

"Now, Dasher! now, Dancer! now, Prancer! and Vixen!
On, Comet! on, Cupid! on, Donder and Blitzen!
To the top of the porch! to the top of the wall!
Now dash away! dash away! dash away all!"

As dry leaves that before the wild hurricane fly,
When they meet with an obstacle, mount to the sky,
So up to the house-top the coursers they flew,
With the sleigh full of toys, and St. Nicholas too.

And then in a twinkling, I heard on the roof
The prancing and pawing of each little hoof.
As I drew in my head, and was turning around,
Down the chimney St. Nicholas came with a bound.

He was dressed all in fur from his head to his foot.
And his clothes were all tarnished with ashes and soot:
A bundle of toys he had flung on his back,
And he looked like a peddler just opening his pack.

His eyes, how they twinkled! his dimples how merry!
His cheeks were like roses, his nose like a cherry!
His droll little mouth was drawn up like a bow,
And the beard on his chin was white as the snow;

The stump of a pipe he held tight in his teeth,
And the smoke, it encircled his head like a wreath.
He had a broad face, and a little round belly
That shook, when he laughed, like a bowl full of jelly.

He was chubby and plump—a right jolly old elf—
And I laughed, when I saw him, in spite of myself;
A wink of his eye, and a twist of his head,
Soon gave me to know I had nothing to dread.

He spoke not a word, but went straight to his work,
And filled all the stockings; then turned with a jerk,
And laying his finger aside of his nose,
And giving a nod, up the chimney he rose.

He sprang to his sleigh, to his team gave a whistle,
And away they all flew, like the down of a thistle,
But I heard him exclaim, e're he drove out of sight,
"Happy Christmas to all, and to all a good-night!"

Winter-Time

• robert louis stevenson •

Late lies the wintry sun a-bed,
A frosty, fiery sleepy-head;
Blinks but an hour or two; and then,
A blood-red orange, sets again.

Before the stars have left the skies,
At morning in the dark I rise;
And shivering in my nakedness,
By the cold candle, bathe and dress.

Close by the jolly fire I sit
To warm my frozen bones a bit;
Or with a reindeer-sled, explore
The colder countries round the door.

When to go out, my nurse doth wrap
Me in my comforter and cap;
The cold wind burns my face, and blows
Its frosty pepper up my nose.

Black are my steps on silver sod;
Thick blows my frosty breath abroad;
And tree and house, and hill and lake,
Are frosted like a wedding-cake.

The Legend of the Christmas Rose

· english legend ·

Legend says that a little shepherd girl of Bethlehem followed after the shepherds who had received the angel's message and were journeying to the stable. All the shepherds took along gifts for the Christ child, but the little girl had no gift to give. As she lagged behind the others, somewhat sad at heart, there suddenly appeared an angel in a glow of light, who scattered beautiful white roses in her path. Eagerly she gathered them in her arms and laid them at the manger as her gift to the little Lord Jesus.

A Christmas Carol

an excerpt

• charles dickens •

Although they had but that moment left the school behind them, they were now in the busy thoroughfares of a city, where shadowy passengers passed and repassed; where shadowy carts and coaches battled for the way, and all the strife and tumult of a real city were. It was made plain enough, by the dressing of the shops, that here too it was Christmas time again; but it was evening, and the streets were lighted up.

The Ghost stopped at a certain warehouse door, and asked Scrooge if he knew it.

"Know it!" said Scrooge. "Was I apprenticed here?"

They went in. At sight of an old gentleman in a Welsh wig, sitting behind such a high desk that if he had been two inches taller he must have knocked his head against the ceiling, Scrooge cried in great excitement:

"Why, it's old Fezziwig! Bless his heart; it's Fezziwig alive again!"

Old Fezziwig laid down his pen, and looked up at the clock, which pointed to the hour of seven. He rubbed his hands; adjusted his capacious waistcoat; laughed all over himself, from his shows to his organ of benevolence; and called out in a comfortable, oily, rich, fat, jovial voice:

"Yo ho, there! Ebenezer! Dick!"

Scrooge's former self, now grown a young man, came briskly in, accompanied by his fellow 'prentice.

"Dick Wilkens, to be sure!" said Scrooge to the Ghost. "Bless me, yes. There he is. He was very much attached to me, was Dick. Poor Dick! Dear, dear!"

"Yo ho, my boys!" said Fezziwig. "No more work tonight. Christmas Eve, Dick. Christmas, Ebenezer! Let's have the shutters up," cried old Fezziwig, with a sharp clap of his hands, "before a man can say Jack Robinson!"

You wouldn't believe how those two fellows went at it! They charged into the street with the shutters—one, two, three—had them up in their places—four, five, six—barred 'em and pinned 'em—seven, eight, nine— and came back before you could have got to twelve, panting like race-horses.

"Hilli-ho!" cried old Fezziwig, skipping down from the high desk, with wonderful agility. "Clear away, my lads, and let's have lots of room here! Hilli-ho, Dick! Chirrup, Ebenezer!"

Clear away! There was nothing they wouldn't have cleared away, or couldn't have cleared away, with old Fezziwig looking on. It was done in a minute. Every movable was packed off, as if it were dismissed from public life for evermore; the floor was swept and watered, the lamps were trimmed, fuel was heaped upon the fire; and the warehouse was as snug, and warm, and dry, and bright a ball-room, as you would desire to see upon a winter's night.

In came a fiddler with a music-book and went up to the lofty desk, and made an orchestra of it, and tuned like fifty stomach-aches.

In came Mrs. Fezziwig, one vast substantial smile. In came the three Miss Fezziwigs, beaming and lovable. In came the six young followers whose hearts they broke. In came all the young men and women employed in the business. In came the housemaid, with her cousin, the baker. In came the cook, with her brother's particular friend, the milkman. In came the boy from over the way, who was suspected of not having board enough from his master; trying to hide himself behind the girl from next door but one, who was proved to have had her ears pulled by her Mistress.

In they all came, one after another; some shyly, some boldly, some gracefully, some awkwardly, some pushing, some pulling; in they all came, anyhow and everyhow. Away they all went, twenty couples at once, hands half round and back again the other way; down the middle and up again; round and round in various stages of affectionate grouping; old top couple always turning up in the wrong place; new top couple starting off again, as soon as they got there; all top couples at last, and not a bottom one to help them. When this result was brought about, old Fezziwig, clapping his hands to stop the dance, cried out, "Well done!" and the fiddler plunged his hot face into a pot of porter, especially provided for that purpose.

But scorning rest upon his reappearance, he instantly began again, though there were no dancers yet, as if the other fiddler had been carried home, exhausted, on a shutter; and he were a brand-new man resolved to beat him out of sight, or perish.

There were more dances, and there were forfeits, and more dances, and there was cake, and there was negus, and there was a great piece of

Cold Roast, and there was a great piece of Cold Boiled, and there were mince-pies, and plenty of beer. But the great effect of the evening came after the Roast and Boiled, when the fiddler (an artful dog, mind! The sort of man who knew his business better than you or I could have told it him!) struck up "Sir Roger de Coverley." Then old Fezziwig stood out to dance with Mrs. Fezziwig. Top couple, too; with a good stiff piece of work cut out for them; three or four and twenty pair of partners; people who were not to be trifled with; people who *would* dance, and had no notion of walking.

But if they had been twice as many: ah, four times: old Fezziwig would have been a match for them, and so would Mrs. Fezziwig. As to *her*, she was worthy to be his partner in every sense of the term. If that's not high praise, tell me higher, and I'll use it. A positive light appeared to issue from Fezziwig's calves. They shone in every part of the dance like moons. You couldn't have predicted, at any given time, what would become of 'em next. And when old Fezziwig and Mrs. Fezziwig had gone all through the dance; advance and retire, hold hands with your partner; bow and curtsey; corkscrew; thread-the-needle, and back again to your place; Fezziwig "cut" —cut so deftly, that he appeared to wink with his legs, and came upon his feet again without a stagger.

When the clock struck eleven, the domestic ball broke up. Mr. and Mrs. Fezziwig took their stations, one on either side of the door, and shaking hands with every person individually as he or she went out, wished him or her a Merry Christmas. When everybody had retired but the two 'prentices, they did the same to them; and thus the cheerful voices died away, and the lads were left to their beds; which were under a counter in the back-shop.

During the whole of this time, Scrooge had acted like a man out of his wits. His heart and soul were in the scene, and with his former self. He corroborated everything, remembered everything, enjoyed everything, and underwent the strangest agitation. It was not until now, when the bright faces of his former self and Dick were turned from them, that he remembered the Ghost, and became conscious that it was looking full upon him, while the light upon its head burnt very clear.

"A small matter," said the Ghost, "to make these silly folks so full of gratitude."

"Small!" echoed Scrooge.

The Spirit signed to him to listen to the two apprentices, who were pouring out their hearts in praise of Fezziwig: and when he had done so, said,

"Why! Is it not? He has spent but a few pounds of your mortal money: three or four perhaps. Is that so much that he deserves this praise?"

"It isn't that," said Scrooge, heated by the remark, and speaking unconsciously like his former, not his latter, self. "It isn't that, Spirit. He has the power to render us happy or unhappy; to make our service light or burdensome; a pleasure or a toil. Say that his power lies in words and looks; in things so slight and insignificant that it is impossible to add and count 'em up: what then? The happiness he gives, is quite as great as if it cost a fortune."

He felt the Spirit's glance, and stopped.

"What is the matter?" asked the Ghost.

"Nothing particular," said Scrooge.

"Something, I think?" the Ghost insisted.

"No," said Scrooge, "No. I should like to be able to say a word or two to my clerk just now! That's all."

Silent Night

• joseph mohr and franz gruber •

Silent night, holy night,
All is calm, all is bright.
Round yon Virgin Mother and Child
Holy Infant so tender and mild,
Sleep in heavenly peace,
Sleep in heavenly peace.

Silent night, holy night,
Shepherds quake at the sight.
Glories stream from heaven afar,
Heavenly hosts sing Alleluia,
Christ the Savior is born,
Christ the Savior is born.

Silent night, holy night,
Son of God love's pure light.
Radiant beams from Thy holy face,
With the dawn of redeeming grace,
Jesus Lord at Thy birth.
Jesus Lord at Thy birth.

The North Wind

• author unknown •

The north wind doth blow,
And we shall have snow,
And what will poor robin do then, poor thing?
O, he'll go to the barn,
And to keep himself warm
He'll hide his head under his wing, poor thing.

The north wind doth blow,
And we shall have snow,
And what will the swallow do then, poor thing?
O, do you not know,
He's gone long ago
To a country much warmer than ours, poor thing.

The north wind doth blow,
And we shall have snow,
And what will the doormouse do then, poor thing?
Rolled up in a ball,
In his nest snug and small,
He'll sleep till the winter is past, poor thing.

The north wind doth blow,
And we shall have snow,
And what will the children do then, poor things?
O, when lessons are done,
They'll jump, slide, and run,
And play till they make themselves warm, poor things.

Day Before Christmas

· author unknown ·

We have been helping with the cake
And licking out the pan,
And wrapping up our packages
As neatly as we can.
We have hung our stockings up
Beside the open grate,
And now there's nothing more to do
Except
To
Wait.

Have Yourself a Merry Little Christmas

· hugh martin and ralph blane ·

Have yourself a merry little Christmas,
Let your heart be light,
From now on our troubles
Will be out of sight.

Have yourself a merry little Christmas,
Make the yuletide gay,
From now on our troubles
Will be miles away.

Here we are as in olden days,
Happy golden days of yore,
Faithful friends who are dear to us
Gather near to us once more.

Through the years we all will be together
If the fates allow,
Hang a shining star up on the highest bough
And have yourself a merry little Christmas now.

It Came upon a Midnight Clear

· edmond h. sears and richard s. willis ·

It came upon a midnight clear,
That glorious song of old,
From angels bending near the earth
To touch their harps of gold.

Peace on the earth, goodwill to men
From heaven's all-gracious King.
The world in solemn stillness
Lay to hear the angels sing.

Still through the cloven skies they come,
With peaceful wings unfurl'd;
And still their heav'nly music floats
O'er all the weary world.

Above its sad and lowly plains
They bend on hov'ring wing.
And ever o'er its Babel sounds
The blessed angels sing.

The Story of Christ's Birth

· luke 2; 1–20 ·

And it came to pass in those days, that there went out a decree from Caesar Augustus, that all the world should be taxed. (And this taxing was first made when Cyrenius was governor of Syria.) And all went to be taxed, every one into his own city. And Joseph also went up from Galilee, out of the city of Nazareth, into Judea, unto the city of David, which is called Bethlehem (because he was of the house and lineage of David), to be taxed with Mary his espoused wife, being great with child.

And so it was, that, while they were there, the days were accomplished that she should be delivered. And she brought forth her firstborn son, and wrapped him in swaddling clothes, and laid him in a manger; because there was no room for them in the inn.

And there were in the same country shepherds abiding in the field, keeping watch over their flock by night. And lo, the angel of the Lord came upon them, and the glory of the Lord shone round about them: and they were sore afraid.

And the angel said unto them, "Fear not: for, behold, I bring you good tidings of great joy, which shall be to all people. For unto you is born this day in the city of David a Savior, which is Christ the Lord. And this shall be a sign unto you; Ye shall find the babe wrapped in swaddling clothes, lying in a manger." And suddenly there was with the angel a multitude of the heavenly host praising God, and saying, "Glory to God in the highest, and on earth peace, goodwill toward men."

And it came to pass, as angels were gone away from them into heaven, the shepherds said one to another: "Let us now go even unto Bethlehem, and see this thing which is to come to pass, which the Lord hath made known unto us." And they came with haste, and found Mary and Joseph, and the babe lying in a manger. And when they had seen it, they made known abroad the saying which was told them concerning this child. And all that heard it wondered at those things which were told them by the shepherds. But Mary kept all the things, and pondered them in her heart. And the shepherds returned, glorifying and praising God for all the things that they had heard and seen, as it was told unto them.

Joy to the World

· isaac watts and lowell mason ·

Joy to the world!
The Lord is come:
Let earth receive her King.
Let ev'ry heart prepare Him room,
And heav'n and nature sing,
And heav'n and nature sing,
And heaven and heaven and nature sing.

Joy to the world!
The Savior reigns:
Let men their songs employ,
While fields and floods, rocks, hills and plains,
Repeat the sounding joy,
Repeat the sounding joy,
Repeat, repeat the sounding joy.

He rules the world
With truth and grace,
And makes the nations prove
The glories of his righteousness,
And wonders of his love,
And wonders of his love,
And wonders, wonders of his love.

Christmas Eve

· bill watterson ·

On the windowpanes the icy frost
Leaves feathered patterns, criped and crossed
But in our house the Christmas tree
Is decorated festively
With tiny dots of colored light
That cozy up this winter night.
Christmas songs familiar, slow
Play softly on the radio.
Pops and hisses from the fire
Whistle with the bells and choir.
Trying now to fall asleep
On my back and dreaming deep
Tomorrow's what I'm waiting for,
But I can wait a little more.

The Snow

• f. ann elliot •

The snow, in bitter cold,
Fell all the night;
And we awoke to see
The garden white.
And still the silvery flakes
Go whirling by,
White feathers fluttering
From a gray sky.
Beyond the gate, soft feet
In silence go,
Beyond the frosted pane.
White shines the snow.

We Wish You a Merry Christmas

· traditional english carol ·

We wish you a Merry Christmas,
We wish you a Merry Christmas,
We wish you a Merry Christmas,
And a happy New Year.

Good tidings we bring
To you and your kin,
Good tidings for Christmas
And a happy New Year.

Now bring us some figgy pudding,
Now bring us some figgy pudding,
Now bring us some figgy pudding,
And bring it out here.

O we won't go until we've got some,
We won't go until we've got some,
We won't go until we've got some,
So bring it out here.

O we all like figgy pudding,
Yes, we all like figgy pudding,
We all like figgy pudding,
So bring it out here.

Christmas Is Coming

· mother goose ·

Christmas is coming,
The goose is getting fat,
Please to put a penny in an old man's hat.
If you haven't got a penny,
A half-penny will do,
If you haven't got a half-penny,
God bless you!

The Snow Lies White on Roof and Tree

· author unkonwn ·

The snow lies white on roof and tree,
Frost fairies creep about,
The world's as still as it can be,
And Santa Claus is out.

He's making haste his gifts to leave,
While the stars show his way,
There'll soon be no more Christmas Eve,
Because it's soon to be Christmas Day!

Christmas Carol

from *The Wind in the Willows*

· kenneth graham ·

Villagers all this frosty tide,
Let your doors swing open wide,
Though wind may follow and snow be tied,
Let draw us in by your fire to bide,
Joy shall be yours in the morning.

Here we stand in the cold and the sleet,
Blowing fingers and stamping feet,
Come from far away you to greet,
You by the fire and we in the street,
Bidding you joy in the morning.

For e're one half of the night was gone,
Sudden a star has led us on,
Raining bliss and benison,
Bliss tomorrow and more and on,
Joy for every morning.

Good man Joseph toiled through the snow,
Saw the star of the stable low,
Mary she might not further go,
Welcome thatch and litter below,
Joy was hers in the morning.

And then they heard the angels tell,
Who were the first to cry Noel,
Animals all as it befell,
In the stable where they all did dwell,
Joy shall be theirs in the morning.

Long, Long Ago

· author unknown ·

Winds thro' the olive trees
Softly did blow,
Round little Bethlehem,
Long, long ago.
Sheep on the hillside lay
Whiter than snow;
Shepherds were watching them,
Long, long ago.

Then from the happy sky,
Angels bent low,
Singing their songs of joy,
Long, long ago.
For in a manger bed,
Cradled we know,
Christ came to Bethlehem,
Long, long ago.

O Christmas Tree

· traditional german carol ·

O Christmas tree,

O Christmas tree,

You stand in verdant beauty!

O Christmas tree,

O Christmas tree,

You stand in verdant beauty!

Your boughs are green in summer's glow.

And do not fade in winter's snow.

O Christmas tree,

O Christmas tree,

You stand in verdant beauty!

The Bells

an excerpt

• edgar allan poe •

Hear the sledges with the bells—
Silver bells!
What a world of merriment their melody foretells!
How they tinkle, tinkle, tinkle,
In the icy air of night!
While the stars that oversprinkle
All the heavens seem to twinkle
With a crystalline delight;
Keeping time, time, time,
In a sort of Runic rhyme,
To the tintinnabulation that musically wells
From the bells, bells, bells, bells,
Bells, bells, bells—
From the jingling and the tinkling of the bells.

Christmas Greetings from a Fairy to a Child

· lewis carroll ·

Lady dear, if Fairies may
For a moment lay aside
Cunning tricks and elfish play,
'Tis at happy Christmas-tide.

We have heard the children say—
Gentle children, whom we love—
Long ago, on Christmas Day,
Came a message from above.

Still, as Christmas-tide comes round,
They remember it again—
Echo still the joyful sound
"Peace on earth, good-will to men!"

Yet the hearts must childlike be
Where such heavenly guests abide:
Unto children, in their glee,
All the year is Christmas-tide!

Thus, forgetting tricks and play
For a moment, Lady dear,
We would wish you, if we may,
Merry Christmas, glad New Year!

God Rest Ye Merry, Gentlemen

· traditional english carol ·

God rest ye merry, gentlemen
Let nothing you dismay,
Remember, Christ our Savior
Was born on Christmas Day,
To save us all from Satan's pow'r
When we were gone astray.

O tidings of comfort and joy,
Comfort and joy;
O tidings of comfort and joy!

The Joy of Giving

• john greenleaf whittier •

Somehow, not only for Christmas,
But all the long year through,
The joy that you give to others
Is the joy that comes back to you;
And the more you spend in blessing
The poor and lonely and sad,
The more of your heart's possessing
Returns to make you glad.

The Elves and the Shoemaker

· grimm brothers ·

There was once a shoemaker who worked very hard and was very honest; but still he could not earn enough to live upon, and at last all he had in the world was gone, except just leather enough to make one pair of shoes. Then he cut them all ready to make up the next day, meaning to get up early in the morning to work. His conscience was clear and his heart light amidst all his troubles; so he went peaceably to bed, left all his cares to heaven, and fell asleep. In the morning, after he had said his prayers, he set himself down to his work, when, to his great wonder, there stood the shoes, all ready made, upon the table. The good man knew not what to say or think of this strange event. He looked at the workmanship; there was not one false stitch in the whole job; and all was so neat and true, that it was a complete masterpiece.

That same day a customer came in, and the shoes pleased him so well that he willingly paid a price higher than usual for them; and the poor shoemaker with the money bought leather enough to make two pairs more. In the evening he cut out the work, and went to bed early that he might get up and begin betimes next day: but he was saved all the trouble, for when he got up in the morning the work was finished ready to his hand. Presently in came buyers, who paid him handsomely for his goods, so that he bought leather enough for four pairs more. He cut out the work again over night, and found it finished in the morning as before; and so it went on for some time: what was got ready in the evening was always done by daybreak, and the good man soon became thriving and prosperous again.

One evening about Christmas time, as he and his wife were sitting over the fire chatting together, he said to her, "I should like to sit up and watch to-night, that we may see who it is that comes and does my work for me." The wife liked the thought; so they left a light burning, and hid themselves in the corner of the room behind a curtain that was hung up there, and watched what should happen.

As soon as it was midnight, there came two little naked dwarfs; and they sat themselves upon the shoemaker's bench, took up all the work that was cut out, and began to ply with their little fingers, stitching and rapping and tapping away at such a rate, that the shoemaker was all amazement, and could not take his eyes off for a moment. And on they went till the job was quite finished, and the shoes stood ready for use upon the table. This was long before daybreak; and then they bustled away as quick as lightning.

The next day the wife said to the shoemaker, "These little wights have made us rich, and we ought to be thankful to them, and do them a good office in return. I am quite vexed to see them run about as they do; they have nothing upon their backs to keep off the cold. I'll tell you what, for Christmas I will make each of them a shirt, and a coat and waistcoat, and a pair of pantaloons into the bargain; do you make each of them a little pair of shoes."

The thought pleased the good shoemaker very much; and one Christmas Eve when all the things were ready, they laid them on the table instead of the work that they used to cut out, and then went and bid themselves to watch what the little elves would do. About midnight they came in, and were going to sit down to their work as usual; but when they saw the clothes lying for them, they laughed and were greatly delighted. Then they dressed themselves in the twinkling of an eye, and danced and capered and sprang about as merry as could be, till at last they danced out at the door over the green; and the shoemaker saw them no more: but every thing went well with him from that time forward, as long as he lived.

Sly Santa Claus

• c. s. stone •

All the house was asleep, and the fire burning low,
When, from far up the chimney, came down a "Ho! ho!"
And a little, round man, with a terrible scratching,
Dropped into the room with a wink that was catching.
Yes, down he came, bumping, and thumping, and jumping,
And picking himself up without sight of a bruise!

"Ho! ho!" he kept on as if bursting with cheer.
"Good children, gay children, glad children, see here!
I have brought you fine dolls and gay trumpets, and rings,
Noah's arks, and bright skates, and a host of good things!
I have brought a whole sackful, a packful, a hackful!
Come hither, come hither, come hither and choose!

"Ho! ho!" What is this? Why, they all are asleep!
But their stockings are up! And my presents will keep!
So, in with the candies, the books, and the toys;
All the goodies I have for the good girls and boys.
I'll ram them, and jam them, and slam them, and cram them,
All the stockings will hold while the tired youngsters snooze."

All the while his round shoulders kept ducking and ducking;
And his little, fat fingers kept tucking and tucking;
Until every stocking bulged out, on the wall,
As if it were bursting, and ready to fall.
And then, all at once, with a whisk and a whistle,
And twisting himself like a tough bit of gristle,
He bounced up again, like the down of a thistle.
And nothing was left but the prints of his shoes.

The Twelve Days of Christmas

• traditional english round •

On the twelfth day of Christmas
My true love gave to me
Twelve drummers drumming,
Eleven pipers piping,
Ten lords a-leaping,
Nine ladies dancing,
Eight maids a-milking,
Seven swans a-swimming,
Six geese a-laying,
Five golden rings,
Four calling birds,
Three French hens,
Two turtledoves,
And a partridge in a pear tree.

The Wassail Song

· traditional english carol ·

Here we come a-wassailing
Among the leaves so green;
Here we come a-wand'ring,
So fair to be seen:

Love and joy come to you,
And to you your wassail too;
And God bless you, and send you
A Happy New Year,
And God send you a Happy New Year.

God bless the Master of this house,
Likewise the Mistress too,
And all the little children
That round the table go.

Love and joy come to you,
And to you your wassail too;
And God bless you and send you
A Happy New Year,
And God send you a Happy New Year.

A Child's Christmas in Wales

an excerpt

• dylan thomas •

"Get back to the Presents."

"There were the Useful Presents: engulfing mufflers of the old coach days, and mittens made for giant sloths; zebra scarfs of a substance like silky gum that could be tug-o'-warred down to the galoshes; blinding tam-o'-shanters like patchwork tea cozies and bunny-suited busbies and balaclavas for victims of head-shrinking tribes; from aunts who always wore wool next to the skin there were mustached and rasping vests that made you wonder why the aunts had any skin left at all...."

"Go on the Useless Presents."

"Bags of moist and many-colored jelly babies and a folded flag and a false nose and a tram-conductor's cap and a machine that punched tickets and rang a bell; never a catapult; once, by mistake that no one could explain, a little hatchet; and a celluloid duck that made, when you pressed it, a most unducklike sound, a mewing moo that an ambitious cat might make who wished to be a cow; and a painting book in which I could make the grass, the trees, the sea and the animals any colour I pleased, and still the dazzling sky-blue sheep are grazing in the red field under the rainbow-billed and pea-green birds. Hardboileds, toffee, fudge and allsorts, crunches, cracknels, humbugs, glaciers, marzipan, and butter-welsh for the Welsh. And troops of bright tin soldiers who, if they could not fight, could always run."

Hark! The Herald Angels Sing

· charles wesley and felix mendelssohn ·

Heedless of the wind and weather.
Hark! The herald angels sing,
"Glory to the new-born King!
Peace on earth, and mercy mild,
God and sinners reconciled."

Joyful, all ye nations rise,
Join the triumph of the skies;
With th' angelic host proclaim,
"Christ is born in Bethlehem."

Jingle Bells

· j a m e s   p i e r p o n t ·

Oh! Jingle bells! Jingle bells!
Jingle all the way!
Oh, what fun it is to ride
In a one-horse open sleigh,
Hey! Jingle bells! Jingle bells!
Jingle all the way!
Oh, what fun it is to ride
In a one-horse open sleigh!

The Sugar-Plum Tree

• eugene field •

Have you ever heard of the Sugar-Plum Tree?
'Tis a marvel of great renown!
It blooms on the shore of the Lollipop Sea,
In the garden of Shut-Eye Town.

The fruit that it bears is so wondrously sweet,
As those who have tasted it say,
That good children have only to eat,
Of that fruit to be happy next day.

When you've got to the tree, you would have a hard time,
To capture the fruit which I sing;
The tree is so tall that no person can climb,
To the boughs where the sugar-plums swing.

But up in the tree sits a chocolate cat,
And a gingerbread dog prowls below,
And this is the way you contrive to get at,
Those sugar-plums tempting you so.

You say but the word to that gingerbread dog,
And he barks with such terrible zest,
That the chocolate cat is at once all agog,
As her swelling proportions attest.

And the chocolate cat goes cavorting around,
From this leafy limb unto that,
And the sugar-plums tumble, of course to the ground,
Hurrah for the chocolate cat!

There are marshmallows, gumdrops and peppermint cane:
With stripings of scarlet and gold,
And you carry away of that treasure that rains,
As much as your apron can hold!

So come, little child, cuddle closer to me,
In your dainty white nightcap and gown,
And I'll rock you away to the Sugar-Plum Tree,
In the garden of Shut-Eye Town.

A Day in Winter

• l. c. whiton •

Through the crimson fires of morning
Streaming upwards in the East,
Leaps the sun, with sudden dawning,
Like a captive king released;
And December skies reflected
In the azure hue below
Seem like summer recollected
In the dreaming of the snow—
It is winter, little children,
Let the summer, singing, go!

There are crisp winds gaily blowing
From the North and from the West;
'Bove the river strongly flowing
Lies the river's frozen breast:
O'er its shining silence crashing
Skim the skaters to and fro;
And the noonday splendours flashing
In the rainbow colors show—
It is winter, little children,
Let the summer, singing, go!

When the gorgeous day is dying,
There is swept a cloud of rose
O'er the hilltops softly lying
In the flush of sweet repose;
And the nests, all white with snowing,
In the twilight breezes blow;
And the untired moon is showing
Her bare heart to the snow—
It is winter, little children,
Let the summer, singing, go!

Winter Wonderland

· felix bernard and dick smith ·

Sleigh bells ring, are you list'nin?
In the lane, snow is glist'nin,
A beautiful sight, we're happy tonight,
Walkin' in a winter wonderland!

Gone away is the bluebird,
Here to stay is a new bird,
He sings a love song, as we go along,
Walkin' in a winter wonderland!

In the meadow we can build a snowman,
Then pretend that he is Parson Brown;
He'll say, "Are you married?" We'll say, "No man!
But you can do the job when you're in town!"

Later on we'll conspire
As we dream by the fire,
To face unafraid, the plans that we made,
Walkin' in a winter wonderland!

Yes, Virginia, There Is a Santa Claus

· editorial in *the new york sun, 1897* ·

We take pleasure in answering thus prominently the communication below, expressing at the same time our great gratification that its faithful author is numbered among the friends of *The Sun*:

Dear Editor—

I am 8 years old. Some of my little friends say there is no Santa Claus. Papa says, "If you see it in *The Sun*, it's so." Please tell me the truth, is there a Santa Claus?

—Virginia O' Hanlon

Virginia, your little friends are wrong. They have been affected by the skepticism of a skeptical age. They do not believe except they see. They think that nothing can be which is not comprehensible by their little minds. All minds, Virginia, whether they be men's or children's, are little. In this great universe of ours, man is a mere insect, an ant, in his intellect as compared with the boundless world about him, as measured by the intelligence capable of grasping the whole of truth and knowledge.

Yes, Virginia, there is a Santa Claus. He exists as certainly as love and generosity and devotion exist, and you know that they abound and give to your life its highest beauty and joy. Alas! how dreary would be the world if there were no Santa Claus! It would be as dreary as if there were no Virginias. There would be no childlike faith then, no poetry, no romance to make tolerable this existence. We should have no enjoyment, except in sense and sight. The external light with which childhood fills the world would be extinguished.

Not believe in Santa Claus! You might as well not believe in fairies. You might get your papa to hire men to watch in all the chimneys on Christmas eve to catch Santa Claus, but even if you did not see Santa Claus coming down, what would that prove? Nobody sees Santa Claus, but that is no sign that there is no Santa Claus. The most real things in the world are those that neither children nor men can see. Did you ever see fairies dancing on the lawn? Of course not, but that's no proof that they are not there. Nobody can conceive or imagine all the wonders there are unseen and unseeable in the world.

You tear apart the baby's rattle and see what makes the noise inside, but there is a veil covering the unseen world which not the strongest man, nor even the united strength of all the strongest men that ever lived could tear apart. Only faith, poetry, love, romance, can push aside that curtain and view and picture the supernal beauty and glory beyond. Is it real? Ah, Virginia, in all this world there is nothing else real and abiding.

No Santa Claus! Thank God! he lives and lives forever. A thousand years from now, Virginia, nay 10 times 10,000 years from now, he will continue to make glad the heart of childhood.

—Francis P. Church

Sound the Flute!

· william blake ·

Sound the flute!
Now it's mute.
Birds delight
Day and night;
Nightingale
In the dale
Lark in sky,
Out of sight;
Merrily, Merrily, Merrily,
To welcome in the Year.

Little Boy,
Full of Joy;
Little Girl,
Sweet and small;
Cock does crow,
So do you;
Merry voice,
Infant noise,
Merrily, Merrily, Merrily,
To welcome in the Year.

Little Lamb,
Here I am;
Come and lick
My white neck;
Let me pull
Your soft Wool;
Let me kiss
Your soft face;
Merrily, Merrily, Merrily,
To welcome in the Year.

Acknowledgments

We wish to thank the following properties whose cooperation has made this unique collection possible. All care has been taken to trace ownership of these selections and to make a full acknowledgment. If any errors or omissions have occurred, they will be corrected in subsequent editions, provided notification is sent to the compiler.

Front Cover   Jesse Willcox Smith. *Good Housekeeping* cover illustration, 1920s.

Front Flap   Palmer Cox. From *St. Nicholas,* 1889.

Back Cover   Unknown. Children's book illustration, n.d.

Endpapers   Unknown. Wrapping paper, n.d.

Frontispiece   Unknown. Postcard, circa 1907.

Title Page   Unknown. From *Bilder und Geschichten,* 1915.

Copyright Page   Unknown. Victorian scrap, n.d.

Epigraph   Margaret Tarrant. *Margaret Tarrant's Christmas Garland,* 1942.

Contents   Oliver Herford. Magazine cover illustration, 1917.

10   Ellen Clapsaddle. Postcard, circa 1908.

11   Unknown. From *St Nicholas,* n.d.

13   H. Willebeek Le Mair. Christmas card design, 1924.

14   Charles Huff. Magazine cover illustration, 1919.

17   A. L. Bowley. From *Father Tuck's Annual,* n.d.

18   H. Willebeek Le Mair. Illustration, 1926.

19   Maj. Lindman-Janson. From *Barnens Julrosor,* 1914.

20   Everett Shinn. From *A Christmas Carol,* n.d.

22   Arthur Rackham. From *A Christmas Carol,* 1919.

24   Unknown. From *St. Nicholas,* n.d.

25   Jesse Willcox Smith. *Good Housekeeping* cover illustration, 1920s.

26   Unknown. Postcard, circa 1909.

27   Victor Anderson. From *Tommy Trot's Visit to Santa Claus,* 1908.

28   Ellen Clapsaddle. Postcard, circa 1910.

29   Anne Anderson. From *The Pudgy Puppy Book,* 1927.

30   Charles Robinson. From *In the Beginning,* 1910.

31   Unknown. From *The Graphic Christmas Number,* 1881.

32   Unknown. From *St. Nicholas,* 1907.

33   Ida Bohatta-Morpurgo. *L'ave,* 1933.

34   Hey Paul. From *Sang und Klang,* n.d.

35   Unknown. From *St. Nicholas,* 1907.